Self-discipline

The importance of self-discipline in achieving your goals.

Lucia Dawson

Note from the Author:

When a certain company hires a "Coach", one of the first actions it must undertake is to measure the workers' capacity for self-discipline and give it a percentage of importance greater than that of skills.

Throughout this book we will explain the reasons for this first statement. But we are not going to stop there. This book is also written to help you develop your degree of self-discipline and, if you don't have one, to teach you how to create it.

Come in and enjoy reading it, you'll find that it's actually more useful than you might think at first glance.

Content:

1.- Foreword.

" Look for freedom and become a captive of your desires. Look for discipline and find freedom".

Frank Herbert

The word Discipline will most likely bring us negative connotations. We can remember, in our earliest childhood, the words of our parents associating that word with our education, teaching us everything with constancy, often moving away from our games. Discipline sounds like effort, sweat and tears. The reason for this is because the whole term is associated with the fulfillment of certain norms and rules of conduct.

But the reality is that this word is not bad at all, at least if it is associated with the second definition we can find in the dictionary:

> *"...control of willpower, emotions and preferences to achieve success."*

What this definition indicates to us is rather the way to achieve self-discipline. If we want to go into detail, we must ask ourselves the following questions:

How far can I go on my own, what is my limit of discipline?

What whims can I do without in order to achieve the objectives I set myself?

We are aware that it is not going to be much fun to work on the achievement of our goals, and therefore, the path can become particularly stressful.

Goethe said about discipline:

"It's not enough just to want to do it, you have an obligation to do it."

"I'm obligated to do it."

2.- What is discipline?

"You can't conquer the mountain. You can only conquer yourself.

Jim Whittaker.

If we follow the description in the Wikipedia dictionary, the concept of discipline can be explained as follows:

"Self-discipline, also known as self-control, is defined as a habit based on perseverance and subject to self-control, which maintains a continuous state of effort or manages to cope with the distractions that lead to the achievement of a goal...".

In order to summarize the whole, we can affirm that discipline only deals with the fact that all energy is necessary to achieve a particular objective, and that this can only be achieved with an efficient working system for as long as it is needed, trying to avoid any kind of distraction that undermines that system.

"Discipline is the surest path to greater freedom and independence; it puts the skills and depth of knowledge at the centre and thus opens up more possibilities in life".

In many cases, laziness can flood you, and just thinking about discipline is unpleasant to keep for a long period of time.

"For me, what allows me to fly freely is an order I must follow."
Julie Andrews

During the course of our life, we will find people who do not stop complaining about their own lack of self-discipline. They have ideas about what goals they want to pursue and start working immediately, or they spend part of their time dreaming about those goals. However, despite the initial emphasis, they do not have the willpower to maintain the necessary discipline to guide them to the end of the road. They soon give up those dreams. The reasons for stopping in the middle of a job encompass several aspects. Too often, the main reason is due to a fundamental trait: the so-called lack of self-discipline.

We can solve the term "self-discipline" and "stress" in many people as a "dull sweat". If we explain it in other words, self-discipline carries with it the obligation to do things. And, honestly, these things are neither fun for you nor do you feel like doing them.

But what many forget is that discipline basically means nothing more than the habit of working things out, even if this work and the time it takes is not among our favorite occupations. Even so, everyone knows that the use of time and resources will bring you closer and closer to the desired goal.

Anyway, there is a question that is inevitable, think the way you think, this is the result: for everything you want to achieve in your life, self-discipline is extremely important, essential and necessary, whether to a greater or lesser extent. So, you should start as soon as possible, without any excuse. Self-discipline means that inner voice which you always ignore because your mind does not want to leave its comfort zone.

To begin with, it is also not necessary to lose one's life immediately to make the change. Making it progressive will be much more bearable. But it is recommended that you start with small daily actions attending to daily matters, and soon the first results will begin to emerge. So, encouraged by the attainment of those small goals through the self-imposition of disciplinary minidosis, you will stop pursuing those short-term pleasures on which you are constantly focused and focus on the long-term benefits.

The results of the practice of self-discipline bear the following names:

- Will.

- Trust.

- Self-esteem.

- Respect for oneself.

On the other hand, the absence of discipline leads to:

- Lack of Objectives.

- Postponement and Delay of Responsibilities.

- Ignorance.

- Influx of Whims.

But there is one thing you must keep in mind: basing all your thoughts on the hope of achieving happiness, so that, without further ado, it will not help you to achieve it. You're going to have to get going to achieve your goals, you're going to have to use self-discipline.

Discipline is necessary in all the activities you propose to do if you want to achieve objectives, especially in today's world, which demands a high level of quality, efficiency and effectiveness. So, if you don't have enough discipline to excel in your core activities, you can easily fail, and your chances of success will be reduced unless you change your mind. It is a personal obligation to comply with a series of measures that lead to the achievement of an objective. These actions define strategies, an order, continuity, the right attitude, will, desire, clear goals, perseverance, etc.

From the smallest objectives to the largest, discipline is needed. For example, getting up early to get to work on time as well as creating an enormous infrastructure of a conglomerate of companies. Both objectives require discipline, only the highest objectives require discipline to be pushed to the top.

That's why it's important to instill discipline in a person's early years. The education of the child will have a great influence on his or her future behavior. From a very young age, he has to acquire positive habits, be aware of his tasks such as school, tidying up with his toys, personal care, etc. In this way, in her adult life, she will be able to observe discipline more easily.

2.1.- What can be achieved through discipline?

Through discipline, enormous goals can be achieved. There is a phrase from the famous writer Truman Capote that says:

"discipline is the most important part of success."

and that's something that deserves to be highlighted. There are people who believe that with talent or great intelligence they will certainly succeed, but that's not how it works. Success is faith, energy and conviction, which is the fruit of discipline. You can have different types of goals: spiritual, financial, loving, enterprising, etc., and it is essential that you apply discipline to achieve these goals.

If you want to be a winner, then acquire great self-discipline:

If you read carefully the biographies of the most influential people in humanity, for example: Jesus Christ, Mahatma Gandhi, Gautama Buddha, Steve Jobs, Nelson Mandela, and so on. You will find recurrently that in some sections it is always said:

"You have developed self-discipline"

because it requires repeated actions to penetrate the spirit into a purpose and be a winner. Discipline leads you to use the power of the subconscious in your favor: all actions aimed at a single goal and carried out systematically are the basis of self-discipline.

The three basic rules for establishing discipline are as follows:

1.- You have to realize that maintaining discipline is complicated.

2.- Discipline is by no means a full-time activity.

3.- There is a multiple reward for each disciplined effort.

2.2.- Tips for developing discipline.

"Look for freedom and become a captive of your desires. Look for discipline and find freedom".

Frank Herbert

1.- Analyze the areas in which you lack discipline:

Obviously, if you do this analysis, you will do it based on the areas that are important to your life. Observe your level of performance in the following basic aspects: health care and personal appearance, financial success, professional development, family life, spiritual growth, etc. Maybe you weren't able to establish a routine of actions that would make you lose weight and stay fit, your relationship with money was bad, and so on.

2.- Determine the causality of the indiscipline:

If you are very overweight, what are the main reasons, if you participate in too many social events, if you don't have a healthy eating habit, if you don't have time to exercise, if you are tied to fast food, and so on. Once you know the exact causality of your failures, it's time to work on a plan.

3.- Start the plan with small actions and take advantage of positive messages:

The will is a limited energy and many people don't know it, so if you try too many changes, you probably won't be able to withstand the pressure and fail. It begins slowly, with small changes that will then increase. The indiscipline of certain areas of your life, may come long, so change is not going to happen overnight, it must take its process.

4.- Apply self-control techniques:

There are several self-control techniques to prevent failure. The initial work is the most difficult, after that, you will get used to it. There are several points you must take into account in order to achieve self-control.

a.- Make a compilation of your routines, of the habits you normally perform.

b.- It's vitally important not to obsess over problems. Although you must maintain an objective attitude, it is not good to think about them 24 hours a day, it will subtract energy from you.

c.- Try changing your bad habits for healthier ones. Eliminate vices and acquire healthy routines, such as improving your eating habits, practice some exercise, enjoy nature, are some examples.

d.- A very effective practice is that of relaxation. Standing in moments of stress, closing your eyes and breathing deeply for a few seconds, helps to regain tranquility and clear mind to follow the path.

e.- Analyze the circle of friends around you, whether their habits are beneficial for your new stage or not, and try to adapt your needs to those habits, avoiding those that harm you.

f.- Acquire habits that also allow you to release tensions. As we have mentioned before, not all day should be devoted to discipline, the balance between obligation and leisure is fundamental.

5.- Practice the new routines until they're solid:

In about a month, a new habit has already gained enough power to be well settled, but until then, you have to endure the difficulty and temptations of giving it up, until that routine is solid enough never to separate you from it again.

"The discipline of writing something is the first step in making it happen."

Lee Iacocca

3.- The difference between habit and discipline.

"A little more persistence, a little more effort, and what seemed hopelessly a failure can become a glorious success".

Elbert Hubbard

If self-discipline is the ability to train one's own impulses, then willpower is the necessary fuel for it.

The word discipline really means shaping or teaching, and it combines positive and negative techniques. When children are disciplined, they are taught behavior, they are instructed before they are asked to try something in practice. You become a role model for them, showing them over and over again what they are doing well, and if necessary, also showing them what they are not doing well.

The effective discipline is to point out, "It's okay" when the child sees it as a stimulus while you doubt. Say "no" when the child touches a plug. Ignore repeated attempts to interrupt a phone call but pay attention to him immediately after patiently waiting for his train.

"You'll never change your life until you change something you do every day."

John C. Maxwell

3.1.- Discipline in education.

There are different forms of discipline, but in general, it is a human behavior catalogued as a certain form of freedom, although it is regulated by a series of laws or rules to follow.

"In an educational institution, discipline may be expressed as behavior in which the student is governed by laws of respect for the teacher and with and for classmates."

A person can be disciplined if he is under a certain form of basic rules of respect; let us remember that the freedom of one ends when the freedom of the other begins; therefore, both the educator and the educated deserve respect. Consequently, indiscipline sometimes appears, either because the educator sometimes suppresses the freedom of the educated, or in cases where the educated man abuses his freedom, leading to a violation of the educator's freedom.

Discipline is a commitment to certain conditions imposed by something or someone, indiscipline is infidelity or lack of respect for these conditions.

a.- When is the best time to teach discipline to children?

Between the ages of 3 and 5, it is presented as the best time for adults to teach the child to obey. This is done intelligently and in freedom, not through punishment. The child should do this by combining this requirement with an explanation of why this is happening, stressing the importance of complying with the rules and procedures.

At the age of 9 or 10, a second phase of rebellion usually arises in boys and girls. This is mainly due to the fact that their critical spirit is born at this age. The child begins to see us with critical eyes and analyzes our mistakes and deficiencies. Therefore, parents must agree with what we are asking for. Remember that the example we are setting is the most important thing.

b.- How to establish discipline?

Establish rules: the rules depend on each family. To establish rules, it is important that both parents sit down and take the time to agree on them.

Challenge yourself and motivate the child with positive words at the right time. It will be effective at first, demanding the things he likes best, and then insisting on the things that cost him the most. Also, strengthen them positively if you follow the rules, too.

c.- What to do if unwanted behavior occurs?

Handle it calmly. Not only does it not help to lose your papers, but it can also make the problem worse.

Analyze the cause. Investigate the cause of the child's disobedience.

Develop a plan for solving the problem, taking into account the various alternatives.

Use problem-solving management techniques. Knowing the child's personality, you should use the ones that best fit the child's usual behavior.

"We all have dreams. But to turn dreams into reality, a great deal of determination, dedication, self-discipline, and effort is needed".

Jesse Owens

3.2.- What are habits?

"We are what we do repeatedly; therefore, excellence is not an act, but a habit".

Aristotle

In each habit there is conditioning, that is, the action is subordinated to a signal perception that replaces the primitive cause of the action (an example: hunger in relation to the schedule).

A positive habit is to create something, while a negative habit refers to the suppression of previous reactions to certain perceptions.

Stimulus substitution is the positive aspect of habit. An act becomes automatic and autonomous as more and more external stimuli are released and contains the necessary regulatory perceptions.

The learning of habits is through training, while the instinctive learning method is done through trial and error. Each acquisition is reinforced by repetitions that facilitate the first achievements and the learning of the following.

While in the case of lower species each difficulty is resolved by successful action, in humans, learning how to overcome an obstacle is solved through memory.

Within the influential conditions in the formation of habits are the external, insofar as the perception of the effect of normal stimulus had to precede immediately, and the internal, such as affective tendencies, will or motivation.

At what age should we start teaching habits to our children?

The habits we will have for the rest of our lives are established, developed and developed in early childhood. Habits help strengthen values and yearnings in life. It is never too late to teach or change habits.

What are the most important habits for your child?

- work, hygiene, rest, saving, time, study, food, saving time.

"I learned that I have discipline, self-control and patience. But they gave them to me like a seed, and it's up to me to choose how to develop them".

Joyce Meyer

How to have good habits at home?

Good habits begin in the most propitious environment possible, so we will point out that the first thing we have to maintain in the house is harmony; that is to say, when we try to solve the problems that arise in our daily lives, they should be solved by the members of the house without shouting, fighting, attacking and insulting. Once we have finished with this point, we will be able to realize all the actions that are positive, that help us, without having a feeling of rejection.

Another important factor is communication, because it leads to a clear and efficient understanding of what we want our interlocutors to understand. If for some reason we do not have good communication, the prospect of a good habit when we delegate a function that deserves it, will be diminished or will fail.

"The discipline you learn and the character you build from establishing and achieving an objective can be more valuable than achieving the same goal".

Bo Bennett

3.3.- Promote good school habits.

The habit of learning is undoubtedly very difficult to establish and fix with our children, especially when you want to intervene in certain everyday moments, such as when watching their favorite program or going to play with friends. Much more complicated when it affects academic tasks, such as a certain reluctance to study, since the obligation becomes an arduous affair for them.

The time needed to do homework becomes a very common problem in most homes, not only for young children, but also for older children.

But for the development of the child it is very important to study for a while after school, because it brings a number of advantages in their education:

a.- Lessons taught at school that same day are much better learned and fixed in memory.

b.- If questions arise about the topic being studied at that time, you can ask the next day and learn it more efficiently.

c.- It is very useful to prepare for exams, since it is not the same to study all the material the day before the test, then simply give it a review to make sure you know what may come out on it.

d.- If a little time is used to do homework, it will not only help the student prepare better, but it will also be reflected in his or her good grades.

However, trying to promote this habit in our children can be very difficult, because first the father or mother must have the will and time to promote this habit, and then, because trying to convince the child or young person is not easy. Above all, if the child in question perceives that his school grades are already good using the law of minimum effort.

"Discipline is the refining fire by which talent becomes skill."

Roy L. Smith

Therefore, an alternative for parents is to exercise a dose of authority, always without going overboard. In order to do so, they must establish rules and limits at home, so that family life improves, and among these rules, one must to know who is the person in charge of organizing, ordering and supervising each marked task. The following suggestions may help you to improve the routines established for the tasks to be performed:

a.- It is ideal to create a calendar for each task: this can be determined by mutual agreement with the children, so there is no excuse later that they have to watch a particular TV show, that they have arranged to go out with friends or another "obstacle". They will know that, at a certain time, they have to do their job.

b.- Have a suitable place for homework: here the child can sit and not lie down comfortably, in good light, never in front of the TV or in a place where he can easily be distracted.

c.- Parents should be interested in their children's daily homework: for these good habits to happen, it is very important for parents to ask them every day about the homework they have left; if that day does not exist, they should read a book or magazine that is of interest to the child, solve problems or do some other work related to their training, so that they do not postpone the hours of work at home.

d.- Help him with any doubts they may have: Sometimes the child or teenager can no longer make progress with his or her homework because they don't understand what to do or have some doubts about how to do it. And if you can't, it's good to have the phone numbers of classmates and teachers on hand who can help at any given time.

e.- Have a calendar of special or extracurricular activities: If your child remains in school during out of the school hours at school for special activities, such as learning another language, practicing a sport or an artistic activity, for example, it will be difficult for the child, when he arrives home, to have enough energy to continue with other marked tasks. Therefore, it is advisable to organize and plan well the schedule so that the work, greater or lesser, if it must be done, is as efficient as possible.

Keep in mind that it is never too late to start if good school habits have not been maintained at home. You will always be on time, especially if your children are young; At first it will cost you all a bit of work, so it is important to be flexible in scheduling homework, it may be changed from time to time for special reasons, or even due to the need to do other schoolwork.

"Children cannot develop a good sense of self-discipline if all the rules of control come from outside".

Babara Coloroso.

As we mentioned at the beginning of the chapter, willpower becomes the fuel necessary to acquire any habit, which in the end will become a very valuable tool to increase self-discipline, but we have to say that it is not an innate trait in our personality. But to have it as the only resource is a poor solution. You must learn to manage this intensity of motivation in an autonomous and progressive way. We will explain it in a metaphorical way:

Imagine a situation where we are a precision watch in the construction phase. If we use all the willpower to put all the necessary gears together, when we get to the point where we have to make it work, we have probably spent all that power, or at least a large percentage of it, so it will be much more difficult to keep it running.

We must go through a phase in which the decisions we are going to make, whether they are of greater or lesser importance, must consume a portion of that willpower. We say this because, often, we will have to take some that we do not want, and we will need our precious fuel to decide and plan the objectives. Being aware of needing discipline will help not only to accomplish them, but also to be aware of what is really important in our lives.

Many people among us often complain about this need:

"Self-discipline, I don't have that, but I could use a lot more!"

It is also relatively common that most people are firmly convinced that other people are much more disciplined than themselves. However, we cannot agree with this statement. Because we would even like to affirm that the cause of these problems is a totally different one: most people do not tend to have enough information to be able to judge correctly what discipline really means. Their sense of discipline is not very pronounced.

Much more often, we also incorrectly catalog the meaning of discipline as a fixed trait in other people. However, we do not stop to think of self-control itself, which we often have completely underestimated.

"If you ask many people to list their personal strengths, they will probably define themselves with sincerity, kindness, sense of humor, creative abilities, courage and other virtues, and even describe themselves as humble. But they will never talk about self-control."

And for the same reason that lack or absence of discipline, and lack of willpower are the most common excuses, it is nothing more than a smokescreen to try to cover up personal failure, and later end up surrendering. But one's own personality, genes or even one's own childhood are not indicators of whether or not that person has self-control. Rather, self-control is about a resource, and like every resource, it must be managed in a specific and efficient way.

4.- Learn self-discipline.

"The discipline of study is to acquire the habit of doing something you don't want to do."

Wynton Marsalis

Self-discipline refers to a person's ability to initiate the actions he or she believes he or she should take to achieve certain goals. Self-control, willpower, determination, care, determination... All these terms refer to the same meaning. The tasks that our boss performs on us at work are not self-discipline, because it is not us who are convinced to perform this task, it is not ourselves, it is a different person.

However, when the person responsible for persuading us to do something is ourselves, then we do need to use self-discipline to do it.

During childhood and adolescence, self-discipline plays a minor role in our lives, as we usually have a "boss" who forces us to carry out activities.

We go to school because the teachers assign it to us, we do our homework when our parents tell us to, and we pick up our room when they scold us because we have it totally untidy.

However, in late adolescence and during early adulthood, we begin to need self-discipline to perform a large number of activities.

It is from that age that the discipline acquired throughout our childhood must come to the fore. If we do not have it, we will be forced to learn how to achieve it. Otherwise, our life will become a real ordeal.

5.- Self-discipline in 10 steps.

"Reading about the lives of great men, I discovered that the first victory they had was in themselves. Self-discipline for all of them came first".

Harry S. Truman

Step 1.- Understand what self-discipline is. The first step you have to take to build self-discipline is to understand what it is. Many people think it is an innate personality trait, a trait that is genetically acquired, and that there are people who have it and people who will never have it. If your thought is directed in this direction, the first thing you have to do is to understand that this is not the case.

Self-discipline is not something that comes out of nowhere, it is not a virtue that there are people who carry in their blood and others who unfortunately do not have it. It is something that one creates and builds by oneself.

Obviously, there will be people who will have less effort to have self-discipline, and people who will have more effort, but we all have the capacity to have it, and we all need to work to develop it.

No matter how little self-discipline you have, there is nothing in your brain, body, or personality that prevents you from starting to build your willpower today. Self-discipline is like muscle. If you train it and put time and effort into working on it, it will grow. If you don't, it will never appear in you.

Therefore, get rid of any thought you have about your inability to have self-discipline because it is not true, it can be had if you invest time and effort in its construction.

"As long as you have discipline, you can be successful. Discipline is what makes you do everything you need to do".

Anthony Joshua

Step 2.- Convince yourself. Once you realize that you have the ability to build self-discipline, the next thing you have to do is convince yourself that you want to start having more. If you don't have it, but don't really find the need to have it, this book is not for you, because it won't help you at all. Motivation is probably the most important engine of self-discipline, so if you have no reason to increase your willpower, it simply won't increase.

Make a list of the times you thought you wanted more self-discipline and the reasons for it. Write down the disadvantages of the lack of self-discipline and the benefits of its development.

Make a list of what your goals are and why you want to achieve them. The reasons you want to build it will be your gasoline. For example, I want to build self-discipline, so I can finish college this year or start my own business in 6 months.

"You can't escape tomorrow's responsibilities by avoiding them today."

Abraham Lincoln

Step 3.- Analyze your time. Human beings have the habit of living in automatic pilot mode, and sometimes we may not have self-discipline, but we don't know why it costs us so much to have willpower.

Analyze what you do for a day and a whole week. Make a list of all the activities you do, and then analyze which of them are productive and which are not.

How many hours a day or a week do you invest in television, how many hours in hobbies, or just entertainment?

It is very important that you analyze your schedules in detail and determine which are the time windows in which your lack of self-discipline is obvious.

When you work, the time windows in which you develop a job cannot be used to increase your willpower, but rather the hours you invest in television or the free time you have. Recognizing the hours in which you practice unproductive activities is essential, as we will use this time to train self-discipline.

"Respect your efforts, respect yourself. Self-respect leads to self-discipline. You have real power when you have both firmly in your belt".

Clint Eastwood

Step 4.- Set Goals and Objectives. Discipline doesn't work without objectives, just as cars don't start without an engine. Before starting the construction, we have to decide for ourselves which objectives we want to reach.

Use the previous exercise and visualize which hours of the day are the best to start developing self-esteem.

For example: On Mondays, Tuesdays and Fridays I have 4 hours in the afternoon, which I will never use for a productive activity, I will use at least one hour a day to start building self-discipline.

Once you've done this, your self-discipline will no longer be a vague concept, you'll have time to prove yourself.

"Our happiness depends on self-discipline."

Dennis Prager

Step 5.- Continue to indicate your objectives. Once you have marked a few days to start the test, you must specify your objectives more precisely. It is about taking your diary, marking the days and time windows that you have previously selected and, in any case, writing down the activity that you are going to carry out. Detail the activity as accurately as possible so that you know what you are going to do as the key time approaches.

Writing "I'm going to study" would be too vague a concept for your self-discipline. Instead, writing "I'm going to study topic 1 and 2 of subject x" will help you think more about what you're going to do.

The more specific you are, the better, because your mentality about what you are going to do will be more concretely focused and your chances of achieving it will be greater.

It's a good idea to start with concrete goals and activities, not too long term. This will make it easier for you to reach your goal, and you will make sure that your self-discipline has begun to evolve.

"Discipline, Work. Work, discipline".

Gustav Mahler

Step 6.- Recognize your barriers. When you reach your "mini-objectives," it is important to identify your barriers and distractions. How do you do it? Very simply, do an analysis of the stimuli that generally cause your self-discipline to fail.

What makes me not start if I want to do something? They can be a variety of things, but if you stop thinking about it, you'll no doubt realize what they are: Watching TV, meeting a friend, being at my partner's house, going downstairs and having coffee...

Think of all the barriers you discover, because as the time specified in your diary approaches, you will have to avoid these distractions.

"Success is no accident. It is hard work, perseverance, learning, study, sacrifice and, above all, love for what you are doing and for what you are learning".

Pelé

Step 7.- Gradually increase your objectives and work times. We have started with very simple activities and objectives, so it is very easy for you to reach them and overcome their barriers more easily. If you complete all the activities marked in your agenda, you will have to gradually increase them.

You need to do it slowly, adapting your skills to the needs that the tasks require. If at any time you see that you cannot increase your goals, stay calm and continue with the goals you had at that time.

Self-discipline is something that is slowly being built up; you won't acquire it overnight. You have to work on it gradually, but make sure you reach the goals you have at every moment.

"Whatever you do, do it with determination. You have a life to live, to work with passion and to give the best of yourself".

Alia Bhatt

Step 8.- Always remember your commitment. Now that your goals are increasing and the hours of the week that are destined to increase your willpower, you have to pay attention not to decay in the fulfillment of the marked schedules. Overconfidence in your abilities can make you fall back into idleness. When this happens, the opposite idea of self-discipline appears, and at the same time you will not be able to achieve one of your objectives, a fact that could reduce your motivation and spoil everything.

To avoid this, I recommend that you set an alarm on your phone every time you reach a goal. Also, it makes sense for you to accompany this alarm with a reinforcement message, such as:

"I'm getting better every day"

"I will continue to work on my self-discipline."

"I'm on the right track to achieve my goals."

Step 9.- Establish your own reward system. It will be much easier for you to achieve your goals when you set up a reward calendar. In the same way, if you get used to doing the activities you like as a reward for your efforts, you'll enjoy them a lot more.

There's nothing better than going to the movies on a Friday afternoon because you know you've finished your work week or having a drink with friends the day you achieve all your goals.

Establish a reward for each week in which you have achieved all of your goals. You'll see how good you feel and how motivated you are to never miss your date with self-discipline.

"Let us guide our students along the path of discipline from the material, through function, to creative work".

Ludwig Mies Van Der Rohe

Step 10.- Be benevolent, but consistent with yourself. Reach your goals, don't leave tasks half-hearted, focus your attention, do things right, don't relax, don't reward yourself if you don't deserve it. You don't have to go from zero to a hundred in one moment, give yourself time, go at your own pace, and if one day you don't reach a goal, don't punish yourself and make sure you don't miss the next one.

6.- The origin of Self-discipline and the use of willpower.

"There are hunters and there are victims. Because of your discipline, cunning, obedience and vigilance, it is up to you to decide whether you will be a hunter or a victim".

James Mattis

Where does self-discipline come from? What is the origin of the use of willpower to acquire self-discipline? To be able to answer these two questions, we have to look back. To go into more detail, we are going to take a time leap of about 100,000 years. So, we are talking about the period around the Stone Age. The daily life of our ancestors, who were known as hunter-gatherers, was surprisingly simple, but equally full of dangers.

1.- Collect and collect food so as not to starve under any circumstances.

2.- To avoid encounters with dangerous animals, as humans considered them potential prey, because the objective was no other than mere survival.

3.- Repeat points one and two. Day after day, week after week, month after month and, hopefully, year after year.

But the tribes, which refined their ability to survive, gained in population over the years, thus providing more security and protection. According to Maslow's hierarchy of needs, this point is essential to achieve a sense of satisfaction. However, with the new stability gained, several standards were also introduced, and with them, certain compromises became necessary:

If the neighbor needs shelter, the commitment that is born is that of cooperation.

Never fight against the members of your own tribe, establish a code or council dedicated to the resolution of disputes.

For the prevention of incest, it is forbidden to sleep even with first cousins.

Preference of long-term relationships to one-night stands: introduction of monogamy.

In order for man to find his way around the increasingly complex society and the development of the tribal economy, he was forced to learn to continually control his instincts.

In other words, self-discipline and willpower are probably born out of the need to support large groups, creating the first societies in keeping with the onset of sedentarism. However, this is only a hypothesis not yet fully demonstrated in a scientific way, based on the evidence found in the settlements of that time. Even so, we will take it as valid until we have a deeper knowledge of the first tribes on our planet.

But one thing we can agree on: until then, self-discipline was never intended to satisfy the abundance of stimulants, but to procure a certain survival status of the human species in the face of nature.

7.- The human brain and its evolution.

"To discipline your body, you need a disciplined mind."

Mehmet Murat Ildan.

Before we begin to deal with what can be considered self-discipline, a small excursion to the human brain is necessary.

Without a doubt, the human brain is the most complex organ in the world, with which scientists continue to research to this day. This complexity can be explained by the fact that the progressive growth of this organism has the greatest influence on the individual, since the human being also constantly evolves. And although it seems that its nature responds to processes of restarting or updating continuous progress, when it comes to long processes, in reality it is a process of new construction of the evolutionary bases. And this is precisely the reason why the brain is considered the most important organ in biological research and in the evolution of the human species.

The area of the Brainstem is the first area of our brain to begin to work and grow, 500 million years ago. From the brain originate the most vital actions of our organism, such as heartbeat, breathing, intestinal activity or food intake. They are the fundamental actions of our organism that allow us to stay alive. All this, everything that happens in this area of our brain, does the same in the subconscious. As a consequence, what we are talking about is a form of happiness, because without the orders that the brain stem emits, we would have to control our breathing and heart beats being continuously pending.

The Limbic System is the area above the Brainstem and is the originator of mammal development. It regulates our social nature and emotions, and certain characteristic actions such as the education of children, but also the feeling of love, the feeling of fear, the instinctive tendency to play or have sex, as well as spiritual development through imitation.

The largest, most developed area of our brain is the Neocortex. It represents the driver of everything we do and is the part of the brain that ultimately makes us human. The multisensory and motor Neocortex starts from the Cerebral Cortex.

The Prefrontal Cortex is the area exactly at the back of our forehead. It is the superior control center of our brain, from where all decisions are made, whether they are more important or more banal, and it is, in turn, where self-discipline settles. Moreover, it is the "I", that is, the part with which we identify when we have to think or judge ourselves.

So, we can prove in the truest sense of the word that we are more than we think we are. But it is precisely this "more," which we don't even perceive exists, that deprives energy in a horrible way, from the very source from which the conscious decisions you make emanate.

"To enjoy good health, to bring true happiness to the family, to bring peace to all, one must first discipline oneself and control one's own mind. If a man can control his mind, he can find the way to enlightenment, and all wisdom and virtue will naturally come to him".

Buddha

8.- Our mental "battery",

willpower.

"Nothing can resist the power of human will if we are willing to risk ourselves to achieve a purpose."

Benjamin Disraeli

So now we know how willpower originated and where it is located in our brain. That's what we're going to talk about next, what willpower is.

Brain metabolism is important so that our whole system can get going. We have to point out that our brain needs twenty percent more or less of all the oxygen that our organism absorbs. The continuous energy input necessary for the function of an adult's brain is only a few watts and a few millimeters of ATP, scientifically also called adenosine triphosphate, which the brain synthesizes every minute.

The brain needs a constant and perennial supply of glucose to provide the phosphates, which are rich in the energy we need, and which we also know as glucose, and is very important also for our muscles, organs and immune system, running through the bloodstream. Stopping this blood flow causes a lack of oxygen and glucose, which leads to loss of consciousness. The renewed glucose becomes a neurotransmitter, which ensures that the information transmitted in chemical synapses causes stimulation from one nerve cell to another.

Although all this scientific explanation is necessary, we do not want to abound in this very complicated area either, so let us pose the question in a simpler way.

Now think of it this way: Imagine self-discipline as a battery full of balls. At all times, the capacity for self-control, that is, discipline, is based on the level of the battery, because the balls that make it up represent our willpower. Next, let's give a name to those balls that make up the battery: Will-Power Bubbles. The battery is discharged during the day, and with much more intensity if, for example:

"Getting out of bed at the first alarm is discipline."

It is difficult for us to get up in the morning and we need a great effort to achieve it.

If we get angry easily when driving the car.

If we do not eat in a healthy way, either by excess or by lack of the nutrients necessary for a reasonable functioning.

If we walk reluctantly to the gym after work.

Even if we put a forced smile on our face, that battery discharges without us being aware of it, automatically. To summarize the above in an even simpler way: for each of the actions we need to do, whether it is physical work, thinking, deciding, it requires willpower and rewarding this to our brain with a limited number of Will-Power Bubbles.

In doing so, it doesn't matter if we consciously force ourselves to perform these actions, or if we subconsciously resist temptation. Scientists have already discovered that unconscious decisions draw even more energy from the battery than conscious ones. One study even proves it: people have to estimate how many decisions they make about their diet at the end of the day. The study showed that an average of 14 decisions were made. However, these are only conscious decisions. Certain measurement methods have determined the true value and we have found that there are 227 decisions we make each day, which means that more than 200 decisions are made unconsciously, although they are not exempt from the use of willpower.

To give a very simple example in everyday life, going to the supermarket to buy food can be quite exhausting in many circumstances, whether it is the amount of food on the list, a large influx of people, or a long wait to pay. These reasons can make us consume a lot of energy.

Not without a good reason, the battery simile was chosen to represent our energy reserves. We can confirm that there are already many studies, showing that any action that requires willpower, and this willpower always comes from the same energy source.

One of the most famous experiments is that of Roy Baumeister. He divided his students into two groups, and both received biscuits and radishes. Only one of the groups could eat the biscuits, the others had to force the radishes down, so the aim was that they had to resist the temptation to succumb to the biscuits. Afterwards, both received an insoluble puzzle; the students who had eaten the cookies in advance gave up immediately after an average of 20 minutes. The rest of the students who had to muster enough willpower to resist the temptation to eat the cookies gave an average of eight minutes. If we compare results, the first group was 12 minutes longer than the other classmates.

Certainly, if you think about it, the difference between one result and another is quite definite. Because if the stock of Will-Power Bubbles were consumed completely at some point, you would stop thinking. That's why our brain has a "smart save mode" system for dosing each portion of energy. This mode is activated as soon as the energy balance approaches a low level. At that point, the brain is reserving and trying to save energy; that is, the Will-Power bubbles. This explains why our brain operates in such a way that it supplies energy intelligently.

At the end of each day, it is normal to feel your energy diminishing, so you only have desires or strength to rest, doing absolutely nothing. If throughout the day you have been using a good dose of willpower to complete all the tasks, there will come a time when the capacity for self-control also decreases. This is what in psychology is known as ego exhaustion.

Keep in mind that willpower is a limited resource. We can imagine it as one more muscle in our body, so we can work on it to make it stronger, but in the same way, when using it, like any other muscle it gets tired.

Self-control is of vital importance. Having a good self-control is going to benefit you in many daily aspects. People who have high levels of self-control tend to relate to other people more easily, the performance subject to self-control is much higher. However, those with a low level of self-control are more exposed to relational conflicts, and their performance falls visibly.

8.1.- How to work willpower.

"What can I do to be successful with my self-control and, therefore, my willpower?"

The answer is simple. To get started, you need to set up a routine to do it every morning.

Think of willpower as if it were the battery of a mobile phone. He charges it at night while he sleeps and wakes up in the morning with the "battery" fully charged. And as you use your willpower to eat healthily, be productive at work and finally do your cleaning round so everything is right, your "battery" is slowly running out. So, you may feel completely exhausted after a long, stressful day at work, even if you've only been sitting at his desk.

However, there are some things you can do to keep the battery longer without completely discharging it. Certain daily habits will strengthen your willpower and extend the "life of your battery". And the best time to practice them is in the morning.

This is the perfect morning routine for possessing unstoppable willpower:

1.- Get enough sleep.

"In the spiritual life, discipline means creating that space in which something can happen that you hadn't planned for or didn't have".

Henri Nouwen.

If you don't charge your "willpower battery" enough at night, you will automatically start with less energy, so it will be consumed faster. Scientifically, sleep deprivation leads to so-called "light prefrontal dysfunction". In this state, the brain is unable to regulate your emotions or attention as usual.

Essentially, this mood is like being drunk, something we can all agree is not exactly the most favorable for our attention or self-control. Thus, we are more likely to feel frustrated when we are working on complicated tasks, which can make us lose our nerves or get angry with everyone around us.

And aside from the popular myth that you need 8 full hours of sleep, there is no exact number of hours that works the same way for everyone. Some people need 10, some 6 and others the whole area between the two. So, find out the right time for you and offer yourself a fully charged battery every day to start at full capacity the next day.

2.- Practice meditation.

"What is discipline? Discipline means creating order within you".

Meditation is the fastest and most effective way to increase your willpower and extend the "life of your battery". Through meditation, you train your brain to concentrate and resist the feeling of laziness. Studies have shown that simply after 2-3 days of meditation for 10 minutes, your brain will be able to concentrate better, have more energy and be less stressed.

There are many myths surrounding meditation: burning incense sticks, singing songs, wearing tunics... Etc. So let's explain what meditation really is.

Meditation is simply the practice of bringing your thoughts into the present moment. We spend 47% of our lives, either remembering the past or thinking about what we will do in the future, investing very little time in having a clear mind and focusing on what we are doing. Meditation tries to do just that.

Meditation is usually done by sitting upright in a room without interruptions, without noises, focusing completely on the breath.

So, leave 10 minutes of your morning routine aside to devote yourself to meditation. After 2-3 days you will notice an increase in your willpower.

3.- Enjoy a healthy breakfast.

"The secret of discipline is motivation. When a man is sufficiently motivated, discipline will take care of itself."

Alexander Paterson

We've all heard that a healthy breakfast is important. But few know how fundamental it is, especially for your willpower. Food produces a chemical called glucose, which the brain processes and uses as "fuel for willpower.

Any food that contains calories gives your brain glucose to work with. But not all glucose is produced in the same way. Sugared foods produce a fast glucose level that provides fuel for your willpower in the short term, but in the long run, it will cause you other health problems.

The best thing you can do is keep your blood sugar levels stable. This will inflate your brain with enough fuel to use willpower all day long. To do this, researchers recommend a low-glycemic diet.

These are some foods with low glycemic index that will give you long-term energy for your willpower:

Lean proteins. You don't need anything refined, just lean pieces of beef, chicken, pork and fish.

Nuts. Especially nuts, which are rich in omega-3 fatty acids, as well as almonds, hazelnuts and cashews.

Fresh fruit. Fresh fruits are preferable to dried fruits, as they contain a high concentration of natural sugar called fructose. As we have already seen, this leads to a high glucose level in the short term. Bananas, blueberries, apples and cherries are some of the best options available to you.

Vegetables. All vegetables will help you achieve your long-term willpower, but the ones that contain the most energy to strengthen your willpower are the ones that have roots. These include potatoes, sweet potatoes, onions and carrots, which will give you a considerable amount of fuel for your willpower.

If none of the above foods appeal to you for breakfast, try looking at them from this perspective. Since you started the day with a good night's sleep and 10 minutes of meditation, your degree of willpower is about to be extremely high. So it will be much easier for you to eat healthily now than later.

I understand that you prefer to start the day with sugary cereals, pasta or another unhealthy breakfast, who wouldn't want that? But if you can enjoy a low glycemic index breakfast, your battery will stay like new and last much longer for the willpower you need all day long.

4.- Practice any type of sport or physical exercise.

"I admire athletes and their high degree of self-discipline."

Seal

We all know that exercise is good for our health, but is it also good for our willpower? To find out, the researchers conducted a study of 24 people who did not engage in any type of physical exercise, aged 18 to 50, who participated for two months. They enrolled in a gym for free and were asked to exercise only once a week for the first month and three times a week for the second month.

Throughout the study, participants were subjected to various self-control activities to see if they were able to resist temptation as they adapted to increasingly tough and challenging tasks.

The results were more than remarkable. After only 2 months of practice, each participant had increased their ability to resist the temptations and, at the same time, to continue with the development of the assigned tasks.

But the benefits of this experiment did not end there, but went beyond the tasks assigned by the experts. Without the instructions of the researchers, the participants managed to: Procastinar less, feel more control of their emotions, drastically decreased consumption of alcohol, tobacco and caffeine, were able to save more money, consumption of fast food and junk food also fell to very low levels, so their eating habits became healthier, spent less time watching television, spent more time learning new skills and disciplines, lowered spending on impulse purchases, fulfilled their obligations within a shorter time than planned.

All these activities were carried out with the usual exercise.

Now, before you start scheduling yourself to train every morning, get up. It is important to remember that these participants only went to the gym once a week for an entire month. This means that they only went 4 times in total during the entire first month.

Obviously, you don't have to go crazy with your training plan. To get all the benefits mentioned above, all you need to do is create a plan that is consistent and not overwhelming. Whether you can train 1 morning a week or 4 days, that's not the most important thing. To see the results, all you need to do is plan a plan that you don't give up.

5.- Find daily inspiration.

"People say inspiration is not permanent. Well, showers aren't either. That's why we recommend it every day".

Zig Ziglar

We have all experienced the feeling of inspiration at some point in our lives. It may have been a story, a speech by a great leader or a friend/family member. When we are inspired, we get a high level of energy that makes us feel that we can ascend to new heights. It's almost as if we have more willpower.

When we see something inspiring, it illuminates the part of the brain that thinks about long-term goals. The neurons in this part of the brain begin to ignite and we feel a discharge of energy as we begin to believe in our dreams and goals.

This basically means that, through the sense of inspiration, not only do we charge our battery, but we get an improved version that can last even longer.

To use this willpower, try to find something inspiring that you can turn to in the morning. This will help you find the willpower you need, even in the most difficult moments.

Let's set a fairly significant example. Jeff Bezos, owner of Amazon, started from the absolute nothingness. While his talent is immense, it took a lot of willpower from when he was very young, working on his parents' ranch in Texas, to building the empire that is now considered his company. Having an image of Amazon or Jeff Bezos in sight will help inspire you every morning, reminding you that everything is possible with willpower.

6.- Give yourself the time you need to get your routines going.

"The problem with patience and discipline is that it takes both to develop both."

Thomas M. Sterner

Stress is one of the major drains of your willpower. Stress releases a chemical called cortisol into the body, which increases anxiety, reduces your energy and reduces your self-confidence. And what is the main cause of morning stress? Feeling pressured by the goals and tasks to be accomplished during the day.

Take the time to wake up, meditate, eat a healthy breakfast, move around and get inspired before going to work. Yes, we know that in the 21st century world in which we live, it is not easy to take your time in the morning or get enough sleep. But if you do everything in a hurry, the cortisol your body produces can eliminate all the extra willpower provided by your perfect morning routine.

So, do everything you can to go to bed earlier, get up a little earlier, and thus take more time to charge a long-lasting battery full of willpower.

9.- Self-discipline in nutrition.

"You don't catch a fish in dry pants."

Miguel de Cervantes.

As we mentioned in the previous chapter, glucose is a substance of paramount importance that needs to feed our willpower, and we only have one path that leads us to produce the necessary one: through food. Glucose is essential to fully recharge the battery or to bring it back to life. Ultimately, our body transforms almost all food into glucose. Because not all foods have the same nutrients, they send glucose at very different speeds and in very different amounts. Rapid energy or "energy boost" is provided by foods that have a high glycemic index. These include, for example:

Fast food (in addition to hamburgers from the most famous franchises, pizza or kebap) although we already know of its harmful qualities.

White bread, white rice and potatoes (which are starchy foods; also chemically called a polysaccharide)

Biscuits or chocolate (sweets, also considered polysaccharides)

Coca-Cola, soft drinks and juices (sugary drinks are also polysaccharides. They are sugars whose carbon chain is long)

But the problem is that these foods can lead so quickly to low energy. Since sugar is a long carbon chain, the introduction of energy is fast, but short-lived, thus biologically more difficult to degrade. Therefore, the "self-discipline" in terms of eating habits that we must adopt here means that, with a healthy type of food, we will be eating foods with a low glycemic index, i.e. healthier, or these foods are good monkeys and disaccharides, proteins and vitamins, which are also much easier for the body to break down. The most healthy and used examples are:

Most vegetables (tomatoes, peppers, cucumbers, carrots, pumpkins ...)

Seeds, legumes and nuts (known would be, for example, chia seeds, cashews, nuts, etc.).

Meat and fish that are lean and have as little fat as possible (healthy variants would be chicken or salmon, for example).

These foods are supplied with a slower energy wasting process but are distributed evenly over a longer period of time and, as already mentioned, are also easier to degrade. Therefore, in order to provide permanent self-control, it is important to be "energy optimized" and to select in a healthy way the food that will provide us with glucose and, therefore, all energy expenditure.

10.- The charging cycles of our battery.

"Everybody starts at the top, the problem is staying there. Lasting achievement is achieved after a long, slow, self-disciplined climb".

Helen Hayes

The charging process of our power battery needs its proper times. That's why it's good for your body to familiarize itself with the sleep routine every night. During this time, your body will recharge the Will-Power bubbles in your imaginary battery by resting so that it can regain all of its energy. One explanation for why you should sleep at night is that willpower is much more efficient in the morning, once rested. Always make sure you have a good night's sleep. Go to sleep early enough. If you are sensitive to light, an eye mask will help you fall asleep without light. Another drawback you may encounter is, if you live in an area where there is frequent continuous noise, earplugs will be helpful in reducing it. A healthy diet and sufficient exercise are also particularly beneficial accompanied by proper sleep time.

With a sleep deficit, either because the light doesn't let you rest, the annoying incessant noises, if you don't sleep because of the bad thoughts that keep you busy throughout the day, and you can't sleep well, the battery doesn't receive full charge cycles and this causes its capacity to diminish or even end up damaged. So instead of 100%, for example, you can only charge 75% or even less.

Moreover, if there comes a time when you have a sleep deficit for a long period of time, say about 2 or 3 weeks (for some for us already after a week, or even just two days, it can already inflict the first damage), the recharging capacity of our supposed battery will gradually diminish, so that the total result of our energy to be able to exert willpower, when we think it is 100%, in reality the percentage will be much lower.

The factor of adequate hours of rest is very important, sleep is key. Many times, for the sake of a good rest, we must make sacrifices, such as not going out at night, or going to bed early to be able to get up early to have enough time to perform your routines. For this reason, people who prefer to reduce total sleep time wake up without too much energy.

There is also the possibility of increasing the efficiency of the battery, and thus increase, in the same way, the performance capacity. It seems hard to believe, but rest, sports and exercise are very beneficial for refilling the battery and increasing its charging capacity. In other words: the energy will be in continuous replenishment. Although this type of refueling is necessary, a lot of willpower must also be invested. We will only notice that energy efficiency weakens at the end of each day. After the period of adaptation of the body, when the routines are fixed, the body itself will guide you on how and when to proceed.

Writing down all your habits is a pretty effective system when it comes to wanting to increase battery efficiency. This statement is always applied according to one law: The more natural and unconscious the action you perform, the less willpower energy you will need to consume. Therefore, your habits are effortless activities such as brushing your teeth every morning, putting on your shoes, or running (without falling, as used to be the case when you were a child and still couldn't walk).

That's why, at the beginning, we must invest will power, spend that battery of energy, in activities that right now cost you so much to do because, as soon as those tasks become a habit, you will do them mechanically, without needing to spend energy. In this way, you extend the life of your energy. Invest to save.

Also, without noticing it, you are investing in self-control and self-discipline. Habit becomes a disciplinary issue for you. We return to the same example: if you brush your teeth every morning, there comes a day when you don't conceive of a morning without brushing them, your acquired self-discipline will not allow you to stop doing that task.

10.1.- Charge the battery quickly.

Performing a quick charge is surely also another option to use willpower instead of economy mode, which recharges you for a longer period of time. But to be able to perform this type of charging, two attributes crucial to success are required:

A fast and, above all, direct energy supply.

A growing motivation from within.

However, if this system is taken too far, the damage that can arise in your body can be significant. Imagine the classic phases of preparing for an exam, which we can still recognize from our school days, and even more so at university: the comfort of coffee, litres of sugary energy drinks, kilos of pizza, fat and chocolate with a very sweet taste... which will result in an extra abundant and rapid energy intake, combined with the motivation behind the test, is one of the most common examples of this rapid and sporadic recharging that we can do.

There are other types of very stressful situations in which this energy behaviour is justified, such as meeting an important deadline for a project, the surprising increase in workload in the position of project manager, in the transition from school to university, when doing a bachelor's or master's thesis under time pressure, or to pass an important test, which otherwise would not allow you to do another one until the following year.

Certainly, everyone has ever done a sprint energy here or there, because definitely, there are situations in life where you simply can not help it. And we can even say that, in many cases, it even makes sense.

But in the long run, such a strategy is very dangerous. Because then, this important expenditure of extra energy rides in combination with the greatest enemy of willpower "stress". The consequent result of the continued practice of these energy sprints will cause the appearance of cracks in the casing of our supposed cerebral battery, inevitably deteriorating its volume of charge. It can also cause long-term damage to the rest of the body, in the form of heart problems, overweight, hypertension or an excessively high cholesterol level that can calcify the veins.

You must be honest with yourself when dealing with exhaustion syndrome, and not pretend to be fine after an energy expenditure sprint, because this load store you have in your brain can be severely restricted due to major defects in the form of cracks, because the energy "runs out". Anyone who has ever faced a depleted battery knows that it can be very dangerous and toxic. So, please, try to treat your store as if it were a treasure, you must take care of it and keep it out of the danger of abusing it, and always growing. If you damage it, your willpower will fall without possibility of recovery.

So, let's give you a little advice: after one of those inevitable energy sprints, it's important to plan a recovery period to avoid "battery cracking". The best thing is to take a few days off and pamper your body: with healthy foods, such as eating fruits or vegetables, and wellness, such as going to the spa, distracting yourself by doing things that relax you, or booking a massage session.

Who tends to be forgetful and can all that we have discussed in this section is forgotten, so we must re-emphasize the two fundamental issues to be taken into account before performing an energy sprint:

Will power is limited.

All the willpower needed to control self-discipline necessarily comes from the same source of energy.

10.2.- Optimisation of the energy balance.

At this point along the way, you must bear in mind a fact that often happens, and that does not represent any failure. Maybe one particular night, after work, your steps will lead you straight home and not to the gym, or you'll succumb to that rich Swiss chocolate at a friends' gathering, or last week's test, in which you were hoping to pass your grade, has stayed the test. This is all part of life, it's normal for it to happen, and it doesn't mean that you don't have enough willpower, or that you're weaker or worse than other people who have achieved that particular goal.

Try to reflect on how you have used your energy, because perhaps it is just an error in strategy, not in your willpower to carry it out. In any case, you should not think that you have wasted your energy. Mistakes serve to learn something new. Yes, you have used energy and it has not gone well, but you can not falter, you know that this particular strategy does not have a good end. Use what you have just learned, and you will see that drawing the next one requires less effort. You just have to balance your energy expenditure. There are certainly three effective measures to optimize your energy balance:

1.- Minimize activities that can deprive you of willpower in everyday life.

For example, don't surf social networks without a reason.

2.- Increases energy measures in life.

Prioritizing the areas or tasks that are most important throughout a day.

3.- Increase the efficiency of your battery.

That is to say, do not make unnecessary detours in the work procedure. Try to finish it as directly and easily as possible.

To bring your own energy balance to perfection, there are dozens of different possibilities. For example, over the next week, don't face all the challenges you've set yourself and see how the performance of your calculated energy battery behaves.

4.- Enjoy your relax time.

According to studies by scientists around the world, the estimated sleep time should range from six to eight hours. During the night, for an optimal rest of your body, the duration of sleep is necessary at least eight hours. To achieve this, it is recommended that you go to bed a little earlier. Or as an alternative, a short midday sleep (20 to 30 minutes) is also recommended. A nap around midday is, by the way, very common in Asian countries and Spain (they love to say they have to enjoy a little energy rest, because the work is very strenuous). If you're working, it's important to check your schedule beforehand to see if it's compatible if you take a nap at midday.

If circumstances do not make it possible, at least try to take a five to 10 minute break every one or two hours of work, trying to breathe fresh air, with a short walk in nature or in the nearest park; drink a glass of water, do muscle stretching exercises. Any activity that disconnects you from tasks for a few minutes will be equally beneficial, so exploit your creative ability to find what can relax you at any given time.

5.- Modify your eating habits towards healthier food.

A healthy diet is very important in all areas of life. You should do this with respect for your body, add more vegetables, dairy products and fish to important meals of the day, and considerably reduce the proportion of starchy foods. Instead of the chocolate bar, replace your dessert with nuts. Distributing a good proportion of study time food throughout the day is much healthier than eating chocolate once or twice a day. Think about side effects whenever you're tempted to eat heavily.

6.- Incorporate sport into your daily routines.

Those who arrive home exhausted and tired at night should try, if circumstances permit, to devote a small amount of time each morning to the practice of any sport. The ideal is to have a combination of rest at night, a good breakfast and some exercise every morning. If circumstances do not allow it, there are always exercise tables that can be put into practice in the workplace, during one of the scheduled breaks.

7.- Maintain an energetic balance or equilibrium.

Between the energy you consume daily and optimal replenishment will result in a much healthier life, a greater ability to meet your daily challenges, the growth of your willpower and self-discipline and, consequently, the achievement of your goals and objectives, both in the short term, as well as in the long term.

11.- Self-discipline training.

"Knowledge is not enough, we must apply it. It is not enough to want it, we have to do it".

Bruce Lee

There are many studies that have confirmed and demonstrated that, with a high degree of self-control, you can also have a much more relaxed life and, therefore, a greater likelihood of success. In doing so, each person gives a series of priorities according to their idea of being happy: giving the greatest importance to the career, building and maintaining a happy family, having security or financial freedom, giving free rein to passions. This depends entirely on the individual, no one can choose for you, or take away, the purpose of your life.

Once you have clear goals and objectives in life, it is important to understand how discipline works. Because willpower, which we have talked about at length before, and self-discipline are very united and are virtues which are not easy to master. So, we'll give you some sort of basic script of how discipline works, so that you can shape it and adapt it to your way of being and your purposes.

1.- You have to finish what you start.

"Whatever you do, do it with determination. You have a life to live, to work with passion and to give the best of yourself".

Alia Bhatt

This is one of the main advantages of any person who has self-discipline, "what you start, you finish". Self-discipline will be the engine that keeps you moving until you reach what you have set out to achieve. As we have told you on other occasions, it is also very important to focus one hundred percent of your energy when you have a project or an objective and focus on it, not to initiate other projects, at least until the first phase, in which you are acquiring a lesser degree of willpower and discipline goes well; and, automatically, work, effort, perseverance, concentrate on the objective and try to distract yourself as little as possible, overcome the pressure of the task to be performed.

2.- Eliminate victimhood from your life.

"They say I'm a hero, I'm weak, shy, almost insignificant. If, being as I am, I did what I did, imagine what all of you can do together".

Mahatma Gandhi

What an enormous number of people have among their objectives to achieve a good economic position, or at least, to have enough money to be happy, to be in full physical condition or to enjoy good health, to work in what they want to be able to travel around the world, but they do not achieve it. One of the reasons they are not achieving their goals is lack of sacrifice.

People in general want everything to be simple, and we want our dreams to come true from the moment we set our goal, but few people are willing to sacrifice the time, money, and welfare of the present for a better future.

People with self-discipline develop this power of sacrifice without realizing it, and are willing to put up with little discomfort in life in exchange for a big reward: Would you stay home on a Friday night to continue working on one of your projects? Well, that's the power of sacrifice.

3.- Focus on acting.

"The secret to getting ahead is to start."

Mark Twain

People with self-discipline focus on acting, not thinking. They know that thinking is good, so they are usually also great strategists. But once they've established their strategy, they're not worried about whether it's perfect, we know there's no perfect strategy. Strategies are only the starting plan, but the path is where it develops, starts now and don't get lost in so much planning.

Yes, it is important to use a prudent time period for planning, but it is also equally or more important to focus on action. Start, even if you know how, it doesn't matter, just get going. Don't let your projects remain in your thoughts, turn into a sea words or a sad paper stored in a drawer. Start immediately.

4.- Develop the ability to visualize yourself.

"Discipline is a gift. The choice is whether to apply it internally, or externally".

Orrin Woodward

There's no way to be great if your mind hasn't seen you're great first. Visualization projects you to the limit of your thoughts; you'll be as big as your mind stops limiting them. People who develop this ability know how to generate a very good vision for their personal and professional projects. Never underestimate yourself, you are great, and we all have our place in success.

It sounds a bit like a coaching ad, but at the moment I'm not your coach, it's not about that, but I firmly believe that you have to believe it to achieve your goal. If you don't qualify positively, don't expect others to do it for you.

5.- Motivation will help you grow in self-esteem.

"Get in a good mood. Don't think of today's failures but of the success that could come tomorrow. You have set yourself a difficult task, but you will achieve it if you persevere and find joy in overcoming obstacles. Remember that the effort we use to achieve something beautiful is never lost".

Helen Keller

If for some reason you think your motivation is failing and you have little confidence in yourself, there is nothing better than starting to train your self-discipline. Start with small things like getting up 30 minutes early, eating a fruit a day, exercising for 30 minutes, or something else that requires effort for you.

No matter how much effort you put into spurring motivation, you'll see that every time you reach your goal, motivation will grow, which is the same as self-esteem.

6.- You will distribute your time better.

"There are no secrets to success. It is the result of motivation, preparation, hard work and learning from failure".

Colin Powell

People with self-discipline accomplish many things in a short time, while those who let their minds disperse fail to complete half of the activities they have scheduled for that day and tend to doubt very much.

A person with self-discipline appreciates his time, makes decisions in favor of what he has proposed at the end. Even in times of depression, anger, or sadness, they come out of this situation faster because they don't allow themselves to waste time.

Surely some people have had to work very hard for their success in life and their achievement is undoubtedly due when the work done is fully completed and they have felt proud and satisfied that they have reached the goal. From then on, there will be few things in life that can give us a drink of bitterness. Above all, because in order to get where we have come from, we have had to go through periods of that bitterness, and based on motivation, discipline and perseverance, we have successfully overcome them.

"Nothing in the world is worthwhile if it doesn't involve effort, pain and difficulty. Never in my life have I envied the human being who leads an easy life. I have envied a large number of people who lead difficult lives and manage them well".

Theodore Roosevelt

But it is also quite common, and this habit often arises in childhood, that we end up surrendering and trying to apologize with a lack of discipline. But if, for a moment, you take a brief step back and are honest with yourself, you cannot pretend to use lack of talent or knowledge as an excuse, because they can always be compensated for by willpower and self-discipline. Whoever achieves it will always achieve his goals in all circumstances. Objectives such as those listed below:

- Do any type of sport regularly to lose weight or to define your own body.

- Be more diligent in your own work in order to be more successful and thus progress or get more money.

- Saving more money, so by spending less, you can afford to get something of greater value in the long run.

11.1.- The deception of skills versus discipline.

"People die all the time. Life is much more fragile than we think. Therefore, you should treat others in a way that leaves you with no regrets. Fairly, if possible, honestly. It's very easy not to strain and then cry and twist your hands when someone has died".

Haruki Murakami.

Willpower, self-discipline, and endurance. If you want to achieve your goal, you cannot avoid these three virtues, even if the goal to be achieved is not very exciting, and the work to be done to reach it may seem difficult.

Resistance means persevering even when the strategy we have outlined is not adequate to achieve the objective. You start over with a different one. If you don't decide to give up the first changes you need to achieve a level of discipline necessary to achieve the goal, you will have to use willpower and perseverance. To acquire a strong resistance, discipline is needed.

We have learned that willpower is limited, that we need to charge our mental battery by creating routines and habits that will ultimately shape our level of discipline. Without the necessary willpower at the beginning, discipline will never exist, nor will we achieve a high degree of resistance. It is repeatedly demonstrated that we have to be strong enough to control our desires and emotions, to lead us to the path of ultimate success. And this is completely independent of the abilities we possess.

We don't mean that skills aren't necessary or important. Obviously, the path becomes easier if you have developed the necessary skills for the job to be done, and that, as a general rule, your objectives will be marked according to the skills you have. In fact, it's the smart thing to do. What we want to make clear is that, with your skills alone, you won't achieve the success you set out to achieve.

Let us take an example: We have before us two budding writers. The first of them has an innate gift for words; as if by magic, their texts are beautiful and structured. During her time at school, she won a prize in the short story competition. Later, he won another one in high school. She saw her possibilities and decided to become a professional writer. She relied on her ability to the extent that she only wrote when she was inspired, possibly a maximum of a thousand words a week. A publishing house noticed a short story published on a social network and ordered a book from her. He was to write a novel of 100,000 words in two months. Obviously, he didn't finish it. She began by lengthening deadlines, postponing chapters, and finally was fired. She had no willpower, no discipline.

"Success is the sum of small efforts repeated every other day, also".

Robert Collier

The second of our protagonists was with the first one to the same school and to the same institute. In none of these stages did she win a literature prize, but she looked with admiration at that girl who, sitting down to write for half an hour, created such beautiful stories. So, in high school, she specialized in subjects of letters: language, literature, history, art history, Latin, philosophy. Outside of class, twice a week, she went to an academy to learn typing, structure and text analysis, and contacted writers trained to study small specific courses in drama, comedy, theatre or poetry. When Friday arrived, all her friends would party at the disco. She, on the other hand, went to bed early to recover her strength, and on Saturday she dedicated it to putting into practice what she had learned during the week.

She developed her willpower, created a strong discipline around what she wanted to achieve in life, and her resistance became unwavering. She is now a renowned journalist, who in her spare time writes successful novels.

Duckwork and Seligman, of the Department of Scientific Psychology at the University of Pennsylvania, after in-depth research, concluded that a balanced dose of discipline usually produces much better results than IQ. The ability to work beating innate abilities.

In a programme involving 300 young people between the ages of 13 and 14 in 2005, they questioned the disciplinary capacity of minors at the time of repeated compliance with high-level orders, and the rational response of behaviour to such orders in the face of instincts, such as access to anger or the need to cry at the harshness of the tests to which they were subjected.

The results showed that six months later, the students who participated in the experiment scored much better, were less likely to be absent, and performed higher than other classmates.

Later, doctors wanted to measure the results of an intellectual skills test with previous tests of discipline and workload. So, they underwent an intelligence test. Strangely, the results were completely nil. The two tests concluded that the students' IQ had a maximum of forty percent compared to the results of the disciplinary tests.

And they were able to draw another definite conclusion, because the examinations with the young people showed that all those who passed the examinations without immediate reward had a greater concentration on searching for a longer period of time, namely, for a period of time long enough to cover the academic examinations of an entire semester. In contrast, students with a higher IQ, who often needed less discipline to achieve the short-term goal, were comparatively much more likely to fail in the long run.

Therefore, a high IQ is not enough for a student to achieve a long-term goal, such as a college degree, or to achieve it more easily or more quickly. For this reason, we state categorically that a certain dose of discipline, perseverance, and willpower is necessary to achieve these kinds of long-term goals.

Intelligence influences success much less than discipline. In other words, intelligence does not depend on discipline. The marshmallow experiment is one of the tests that has become a benchmark in social psychology.

In these studies, a child was offered a choice between a small immediate reward or two small rewards (i.e., a larger late reward) if they waited a short period of about 15 minutes. During this period, the investigator leaves the room and then returns. The reward was sometimes a marshmallow, but often a cookie or pretzel. In subsequent studies, the researchers found that children who were able to wait longer for the prize have on average better results in their lives in various aspects.

The goal of this test is to demonstrate with the result that the more self-control capacity, the greater the likelihood of achieving long-term goals. This is a fact that can be tested with a child. Following the same parameters, Daniel Golemann, who was a professor at Harvard University, developed a work on emotional intelligence in the mid-1990s, becoming a bestseller. The thesis stated that:

"To succeed, it takes more than a higher level of intelligence. It can be the best of the twenty percent impact in achieving happiness and success throughout life. But those who are able to control their desires, feelings and expectations from the point of view of

patience and consistency will achieve far more success than a person who uses only their intelligence".

We must also say that this test is not a panacea that works in 100 per cent of cases. Dr. Celeste Kidd, a professor at the University of Rochester, studied cases in a home for dysfunctional families in the city of Santa Ana, California. There she saw that the children living in this facility were in misery, and immediately accepted the fruit pieces. In this case, we can say that it is the result of constant denial, and therefore this decision that the other test would have been considered as the fruit of impatience is, in this case, impatient but rational. In a later study by Dr. Kidd, he concluded that the environment in which one lives has a decisive influence on the acceptance of immediate satisfaction.

11.2.- What gets in the way of your own goals?

"Give it light and the darkness will disappear by itself".

Erasmo

Internal barriers are obstacles that stand in our way and prevent us from moving forward, but since we cannot always see and accept them, they are more difficult to overcome. Don't let these obstacles put you in a situation that you don't want, learn to overcome them and increase the well-being and satisfaction of your life.

Internal obstacles are those personal qualities that prevent us from acting in accordance with our desires, limiting us, not allowing us to develop as human beings, and moving away from happiness and emotional and spiritual well-being.

Each person has his or her own inner obstacles. To overcome them, you will also have to use a little willpower. Willpower is the inner impulse that leads us to overcome these obstacles and achieve our goals. It is not something we are born with or not born with. We can develop it and strengthen our willpower if we understand what it is and why we have not done it before. Some of the internal barriers we may have are mainly:

1.- Failure to state reasons. The word motivation comes from the word "motive", which means motor or something that generates movement. Therefore, being motivated means having a reason or desire that leads to action. This desire must become your starting point. But it is essential that you project this desire with intensity, with your mind and heart, with all your strength. That's why it has to be the most important thing for you, and only then will you be ready to make the necessary efforts. We all have two basic sources of motivation:

a.- The motivation that comes from within, from our goals, from the meaning and direction we want to take in life, from our dreams and hopes.

b.- The motivation that we will find in our environment, a motivation that comes from outside, of the possible rewards that society is going to offer us: money, fame, attention, recognition and admiration of others, etc.

This motivation that comes from the outside is the most likely to tempt us to distract our level of discipline, and many people believe that it is the most influential or the only one that exists. External motivation is as good as it is important, but internal motivation is essential.

2.- Little resistance to frustration or failure. Tolerating frustration allows us to face the obstacles that stand in the way of success in life. Low tolerance of frustration leads to anger, depression, and an inability to solve problems with solvency, and leads to avoiding those problems by leaving them unresolved, which will undoubtedly lead to true failure.

3.- Fear of change. Fear of change is something we have all experienced on more than one occasion, and it is difficult to overcome, but it is not reason enough for it to become the feeling that determines our lives. We can be in control by working on our routines of self-control and relaxation. Change can scare us because we don't know how to deal with new situations or situations that take us out of our comfort zone, or because it can lead to some kind of loss, whether physical, moral, emotional, etc. Another reason is the fear of making mistakes and being criticized by others and/or ourselves. We may also be afraid of the lack of self-control that we may feel in certain situations.

4.- Fear of success. It is hard to believe that there is a fear of success, but it is one of the main reasons for our failures and may limit our abilities. Success will frighten us when we believe that our triumphs show our worth as human beings. If we think in this way, when we have reached a certain level of success, we believe that we must maintain it at all costs so as not to lose this acquired status, which would mean being successful in everything we do.

I never usually fail, it is impossible. Faced with this misconception, many people prefer to stagnate at a point that is comfortable for them, where it is easy to surrender. Moreover, they tend to believe that the greater the success, the greater the responsibility, work and effort to be done, and it weighs heavily on them like a rock.

We believe that success requires that we behave as we are, without taking on other responsibilities beyond those we already have, since we run the risk of not being able to handle them. If we think before achieving success that the costs will be very high, we can invade the vertigo and slow down. We have the mistaken belief that we do not deserve success or that we will be unable to sustain it. This will lead us to think that we can lose everything at any moment and, therefore, to suffering.

We also tend to believe that our success will cause envy and discomfort among the people around us, changing or deteriorating our relationships. Relationships we don't want to lose.

We believe that when we achieve our goal, we lose motivation, or we can no longer fight for something. Therefore, from these reflections a question arises:

"What is the reason why people achieve their goals the way they would have liked?"

The answer to this question is generally based on one of the following three reasons:

a.- Impatience. We want to achieve something, and we want to do it immediately. In most cases, this system doesn't work. Impatience here is a factor that plays against us. In fact, we can trace a strategy that tries to fulfill the objective in a determined term of time, that this is the correct one, that we are developing it in an adequate way, but we must be patient because we do not always correct with the times, or inconveniences arise that can delay the arrival to goal.

b.- Distraction. Unfortunately, this is one of the biggest problems that derail plans in our modern times in which we live. The quantity of elements that can distract us, and that we have so close at hand, such as the Internet, television, video games, etc., present 24 hours a day, 365 days a year, can make us confuse our periods of rest, lengthening them in such a way that, in reality, we are only wasting time. Distractions take us away from the objective, they take us out of our routine of discipline if we do not use them with the same discipline with which we face the work.

c.- If you embrace too much, it's quite likely you won't finish anything. It is one thing to carry out the scheduled tasks in their entirety and devote all your time exclusively to finishing them but be prudent with the number of them. No one is able to be in several places at the same time. Suddenly, a new idea comes up that leads you to the next goal, you think you've got the work you're currently doing under control, and you dive into the other task. However, we repeat again, no matter how much we think that everything is under control, at any moment an obstacle can arise, by own or other people's causes, and we don't manage to finish either of the two tasks.

11.3.- What is important and what is needed for self-discipline.

"Don't let mental blocks control you. Be free. Face your fear and turn mental blocks into building blocks".

Roopleen

We have explained in detail the barriers that stand in our way to achieve an objective. This may lead us to ask how is it possible to maintain greater self-discipline in these circumstances? At this point, we are going to find three determining factors that will help us resolve the question:

1.- Have the objective clearly defined. Setting priorities is essential. Set yourself the goal you want to achieve, either in one go, because it's small, or fight battles until you win the war. Properly plan the strategy to follow, put it into practice as soon as possible, without wasting too much time, do not discourage yourself in the face of adversity that will surely appear along the way. If you are clear about where to go and how to get there, we are sure that sooner or later you will make it. Always remember: willpower, discipline, endurance.

2.- Assume full responsibility for the decisions taken and actions taken to put them into practice, whether they go well or not. It won't do any good if you throw balls out, blaming others or simply the elements. It is necessary to analyse where your mistake comes from and how to solve it. Undoubtedly, we all live to some extent depending on third parties, certain articles or events, such as work or family, and that is undoubtedly a positive factor and support in most cases. After all, human beings are social beings. But as a single person, we alone create those dependencies, and their limit, so that the final decisions will always be made by oneself. This means that no matter what we do, it is up to us to take full responsibility, not to delegate to others something that belongs to us.

3.- Use self-motivation through your achievements. The great objective is clear to you, you can visualize it. Of course, getting there can take weeks, maybe months. That's why partial success is necessary. It's important to check with every little achievement if you're still on the right track. If that is the case, then you should reward yourself for it. These small rewards, which seem to be unimportant, are the ones that keep motivation high and bring you closer to final success step by step.

11.4.- Training your self-discipline.

"Never give up. It's like breathing. Once you give up,
your flame dies and let the darkness eradicate every
ounce of hope. You cannot allow it. You must continue
to breathe, even if they are shallow breaths. Keep
trying, even a little so that your dreams don't die.
Never, never, never surrender".

Richelle E. Goodrich

As you will see, self-discipline begins to become a living being within your brain. Therefore, it must be nourished and it must remain active, if you want it to stay in shape. Therefore, there are a number of exercises that help you gain in efficiency. In order for it to work, you must be persevering, so it will end up becoming just another routine, and your self-discipline will become more and more powerful.

Once a week, devote a few minutes of the night, just before your break, to defining a small project to be carried out the next day. It's important that it's not one of your favorite activities, one of those that you usually postpone. To avoid postponing it again, it is important that you write down this project and give it form. To reinforce the obligation to comply, tell your partner, your parents, or a friend, so that this action will create a little pressure on you.

If you manage to start the project, or even finish it, you can give yourself a small reward, according to the magnitude of the achievement. An extra walk at night, enjoy a glass of wine at the end of the day. Something simple, but that motivates you to project another unpleasant task for you. However, if you don't get the project off the ground consistently or don't finish it, don't punish yourself either. In this case, you should try again and again; the more beginnings you make, the more often you will succeed.

In addition to this simple exercise, there are many more to shape your self-discipline. For example, you can get out of your comfort zone once a day. Always with simple actions. If you are shy or unsociable, try greeting a stranger once a day. If you are lazy when doing household chores, try to make the bed or wash the dishes.

11.5.- How your self-discipline evolves.

We already know that we will only find one possible way to achieve our long-term projected goals, we have been learning over the course of this book:

"Discipline, personal motivation and consistency"

One of the decisive factors to advance along the path of discipline is that little by little, you will find the answers yourself without the need for help.

Establishing the first habits and daily routines is very hard. That's where willpower begins to work. Once those first tasks become everyday, the energy you've been using to get them going will be available again.

It's when you realize that it hardly costs you any effort to do what a month ago seemed impossible to you. You have found an answer for yourself. It's the moment of the game when motivation comes into play.

Once motivated by what has been achieved, your willpower capacity has grown, and you set yourself a goal of greater magnitude. You already know how it works, so all the machinery starts up again.

In the end, it's like a snowball falling down the slope of the mountain: it's getting bigger, faster, more powerful. The obstacles in its path become smaller as the ball grows and increases its resistance.

Each factor is a small piece of that unstoppable machine you're building: willpower, habit, discipline, reward, motivation, endurance. The final consequence can be no other than success.

It was passed on to us by our parents when we were children, and now it is we who keep telling our children: discipline is the most important virtue. Because without diligence (that is, here we understand it as discipline) there is no reward. The problem is that discipline is very vilified in these times, it's like the old military marches. Surely the root of the word can't be a little bit to blame for that, because if you take a closer look at the definition, the term "discipline" comes from a dead language, Latin, and means breeding, order, and instruction.

Most researchers, however, agree that discipline is a key success factor. So it's not about whether you just have some qualities that help you achieve success, like innate skills, good training or intellectual skills, you also need to have discipline. However, you already know the good news: while self-discipline isn't exactly the easiest quality to acquire, you can learn. Let's admit that the word "discipline" sounds unsympathetic and "annoying whistles. Discipline sounds like: chain, drill, a barrage of rules, blind obedience, or continued, sustained effort.

Obviously, since no one likes this, because it sounds like a great effort to be made, you will always listen to advice such as:

"Do what you love, and money and success will follow you".

Sure, that sounds much better, but it's just the summarized version you'll find in the Readers Digest of a classic wisdom of success. Because the full version you have to listen to is, rather, something like this:

"Do what you love. Work hard, very hard. Be passionate, determined and open to new things. Interact more than you are asked to do, show discipline, be tenacious, simply persevere and work so hard and a little harder. For then one day money and success will follow you".

This statement is not so famous, because it is known that, without consistency, a lot of work and all this carried out in a disciplined manner, it is impossible to achieve great goals. The myth of:

"How I became a millionaire with little effort "

is completely false. It is very easy to talk when you have reached the dome without remembering that you have walked through the basement before. In this case, it is because we may tend to ignore the whole process that has led us to success, the bad times, the difficulty in making ends meet, the sacrifices of the past, and yet always having maintained an iron discipline, as well as a continuous commitment and bomb-proof perseverance. Many firmly believe that talent is often unevenly distributed, but this is by no means the case or a valid excuse, because the difference is made by diligence, perseverance, and discipline.

Who among you knows the 40% Navy Seals rule? It reads as follows:

"If you think it's no longer possible, you've only achieved 40% of your own performance. It is not your own physical condition that decides, but your mental aptitude."

What this rule says is that every probability of success is based on your degree of discipline. It doesn't depend on other people or methods, it depends exclusively on you to improve your performance and achieve the goals you set. Yes, if you think about it, you can become the absolute master of your destiny, with the invaluable help of discipline.

12.- The dangers of self-discipline.

"Don't look for mistakes, look for the solution".

Henry Ford

Being good at your job, what you do and maintaining discipline is dangerous and almost nobody knows it. There are a number of studies conducted at Duke's Business School that have shown that while self-imposed discipline has many positive points, it also has its drawbacks. People who impose a strong self-discipline end up frustrated when they compete against themselves.

Another danger is that third parties instinctively impose higher demands on these people, because they know that their own disciplinary condition will not allow them to leave the project half-heartedly.

Finally, there is a common characteristic for people who prescribe a very high dose of discipline and reflection for all their actions. They also make a brutal level of demands. This quality arises because, for the sake of their innate capacity, they are accustomed to discipline and, therefore, work many more hours than others, much harder, to the point of exhaustion, becoming slaves to their own self-impositions.

Through a strong discipline, the work never ends, you are never completely satisfied, you can always go one step further, one meter further, regardless of the degree of exhaustion, and overcome any limit of physical and mental endurance. For this reason, self-discipline must be measured in a balanced way without compromising your health.

13.- A summary of what has been learned.

"Whenever you are asked if you can do a job, answer Yes! And start learning how to do it right away."

Franklin Delano Roosevelt

First of all, we will remember that discipline is not innate in us, but is based solely on our capacity for willpower. And it is precisely our willpower that can be trained.

But before starting the plan of operation, it is important to calibrate the level of knowledge and self-control of each one: all of us have power over ourselves and the responsibility to decide how to change things.

The key question is whether you take enough interest in yourself, whether you know what you want and how to get there, as the English proverb rightly states:

"Who's driving the bus? Who's driving, he's the one who's driving the control".

There are many people who prefer to be managed by other people, by so-called "leaders". But those who really want to achieve the objectives by themselves will always find a way or an answer. If you don't want something, you'll find reasons why the project can't succeed. In this case, leave the driver's seat and let the other bus drive, and continue to take refuge in excuses, circumstances, and so on.

There are many ways to see discipline in everyone's daily work, such as those who have the habit of running out every morning, or who are able to overcome adversity when pursuing their goal, all this, always, through discipline. Obviously, there are times when there are doubts that the person, even if disciplined, wonders how to avoid problems. To remain motivated, no matter how tired they are, no matter how many rejections they experience, or suffer the lack of time to complete tasks.

For example, you could use the time, instead of going back and forth in bed in the morning and then blame her, putting sports things in your backpack and practicing some sports just before work begins. That's when the excuses appear immediately, following the trail of the bad conscience, in the form of statements similar to these: I don't have time, I always have work to do, I have to attend this event, today it's bad weather to go for a walk, I don't feel like doing sports. Instead of showing discipline, one tries to throw a pious lie about one's own behavior: I can't do anything about it right now, but next time, I will definitely do it?

There are also those who try to convince themselves that self-discipline is boring and spoils fun. But we cannot deceive ourselves, which would be absurd, because then we must sincerely acknowledge that it is unpleasant that we have to postpone certain tasks, regardless of their size.

In addition, tasks will not be performed by themselves or from the air. There are many people who are overwhelmed by the fear of failure, but are unable to take on jobs that can be challenging, only because they need a good dose of discipline to perform them. The situation automatically leads them to think of failure. All the fears that hide in their minds are more powerful than the mere thought of practicing discipline, and just thinking about it leaves a bad taste in their mouths.

We are sure that you can change all that configuration, always on the basis of discipline, because what distinguishes successful people from the rest of people who are not successful? The difference is, no doubt, that they do not decline in their attempts, they always continue, no matter how difficult it is to exercise discipline.

One of the most famous examples we can show of discipline and failure is that of Abraham Lincoln, one of America's most revered presidents. But what is less well known about him are his beginnings, full of failures and resistance to them:

"But I was ignorant of many things. I could read, write and count, and even the rule of three, but nothing more. I never studied in a school or academy. What I have in the field of education I have been gathering here and there, under the demands of necessity.".

At the age of 22, he already had his own company, a mill warehouse in New Orleans, but failed as a trader. Later, already dedicated to politics, he had to resign his seat as a congressman, opposing the intervention of the United States in Mexico.

He was not discouraged, and was one of the founders of the Republican Party. However, he lost the battle of the internal election for his country's vice-presidential candidate. This new failure only spurred him on, until he finally managed to run for president in 1860.

At the age of 51, he achieved his goal, was elected president of the United States, and entered the history books with full rights. Only he could survive so many defeats to reach the desired goal. Presumably, most people would have already hung up their careers somewhere after the second or third political defeat, and would have retired from public life. But Abraham Lincoln continued, and demonstrated that, with iron discipline, you can get what you set out to get.

There is another study by Dr. Loran Nordgren, professor at Kellogg Business School, in which he concludes that it is necessary to know how to maintain the self-discipline of temptations at a distance. Both terms are counterproductive. The person who wants to achieve a greater degree of self-control must learn to deal with temptations that are nothing more than dissuasive elements of the discipline.

It has also been shown that people who surely believe they have a great capacity for self-control are the most likely to be defeated by temptations.

14.- Conclusion.

This may seem paradoxical now, but many people who consider themselves self-disciplined will never recognize it on their own. Already in the early hours of the morning, out of bed, just to go to work, is for these people as natural as morning brushing. The real challenge is how to get there. How can this be achieved? With the classic steps that are going to make it possible to regulate other things, as if it were a chain:

1.- Act on your own initiative.

Here it is important to first take a step back and ask yourself the question of why you want to establish this project or that as a priority goal. If the desire to achieve something comes from oneself, it is like well-intentioned advice from a third person, that is, practically from the outside. And for resistance to be permanent, it is necessary to recognize all the meaning behind work and effort. It must be one's own desire, otherwise everything else will not work in the long run.

2.- Set your priorities.

Everyone needs to know how to make decisions about their priorities in order to distinguish between tasks that must be done first because of their importance, and those that are not so urgent and can be left for later. And those decisions must be made by yourself. This is where to-do lists are adequate to keep an order of importance.

3.- Set a specific date for completing tasks.

Once you have the goal set, it's important to set an end date. In this way, you will concentrate and dose the effort in such a way that, after the deadline you set at the beginning, you will be able to finish it without having to suffer extra pressure due to lack of time, and, consequently, fail right at the end. You haven't swum so much to die on the beach now.

4.- Decompose large tasks into smaller units.

This works just like with the classic law of inertia, which is known from physics lessons already at school: If a heavy body is set in motion first, it will be easier for it to stay in motion. There is also a very intelligent Chinese proverb that says that all journeys, even the longest imaginable journeys, begin with one step, one simple step. So start with small steps, so it will be easier for you to reach the biggest steps.

5.- Set goals that don't exceed reality.

There is a possibility that you may fail from the beginning, as you may have set goals that are impossible (at least for normal mortals) to achieve. The moment you realize for yourself that your goal is not sustainable at all, frustration builds up and you give up on your goals. At first, it's best to set smaller goals, such as running for 10 minutes every day, because running for 1 hour, if you're not used to it, is going to be impossible. It is precisely at this moment, when you experience a reassuring experience of success, that the goal is most easily achieved.

6.- Find your own personal rhythm.

During the day, each person has different performance phases. At this point, there is a discipline that is considered essential. This is chronobiology. In order to give a more understandable explanation, let us assume that our organism, with all its functions and properties, such as its own metabolism, and all the work of each individual organ that forms it, or, for example, the degree of concentration, varies considerably over the course of an entire day. There are people who do not need to bother getting up at dawn each morning and immediately reach an optimal level of concentration, and those who need to get up after lunch, but instead can concentrate until the early hours of the morning. Each organism is a world and needs some very different rest periods.

The individual power phases of these two types can oscillate drastically over time, because the distribution of energy is established differently. Therefore, each person must know when to activate their personal maximum performance phase in order to work efficiently.

7.- Visualize your own goal.

To get the feeling of motivation needed to perform an act of willpower, you need a strong reason and it is neither more nor less than the possibility of getting a final prize if you achieve the goal. Your leivmotiv, it is worth it to redo it, it is the reward, which causes a positive feeling in the person. This must be clear to everyone. Why do I do everything? What do I give myself after this work has been done? The answer to those questions is enough for some people to imagine the objective; others need a visual representation, that is, an image. So it's best to check what works best for you.

8.- Choose a role model.

Indeed, the very notion of self, which has of itself as a disciplined person, will encourage in your mind for self-discipline to become more intense. In fact, in an essay by Michelle van Dellen, a social psychologist at the University of Georgia, and a classmate at Duke University, Rick Hoyle, we see a person who is looking for two different kinds of food. Food, whether it's a cookie or a carrot. Those who were seen as vegetable-eaters were more self-disciplined later. So, please choose a role model to watch out for and help you be more disciplined.

9.- Ignore unbelievers immediately.

Everyone has ever experienced it on their own: You tell an acquaintance, friend or family member details about your idea and the reaction you encounter is skepticism. The consequence of this is that doubt arises and motivation falters. Before you even understand what's going on, the new project has already flown away. It's better to trust your possibilities and let the naive, skeptical and haters slip you.

10.- Reward the partial successes you've achieved.

Most people tend to reward themselves in advance as soon as there are no positive comments. On the other hand, appreciation has an enormously positive effect. This was proven, for example, in a study by Albert Bandura, professor of psychology at Stanford University. After the experiment, people who were praised became more committed to higher goals and more motivated to accomplish something than others who were not praised. You will feel more committed and even feel that your abilities grow, as well as improving performance if, from time to time, you praise yourself. In other words, everyone should silently praise each other and reward each other for what they have done themselves. Because even this property is shared by all people who are very successful: they try to create as little space as possible between what is to be done and the execution of what is intended and thus add the fun component.

Already Friedrich Nietzsche, one of the most controversial philosophers, once said:

"Many are very persistent on the path they have chosen. However, very few of them are equal in finish".

This means that, in spite of all the vicissitude you will find on the way, there is no possibility of throwing in the towel. There are no shorter or easier ways, you have to follow the marked ones.

Other titles by Lucía Dawson: